*soul*iloquy WITH A traveller

notionpress.com

*soul*iloquy WITH A traveller

SHANTHA

notionpress.com

Notion Press

Old No. 38, New No. 6

McNichols Road, Chetpet

Chennai - 600 031

First Published by Notion Press 2016

ISBN 978-93-5206-704-6

Contents

Preface

Why 'Souliloquy with a Traveller?'

It began because the ramblings in my head would not stop.

It was as if something inside was goading me, telling me that I must keep talking, for talking is healing. The circumstances were truly such that I needed this healing.

The question rose then, who was giving me these words? I was relating my life experiences – but it was as if it was the voice of someone else, through the medium of a person not entirely me. This 'person' then, has to be my soul, for there is no one else. This then, is the 'traveller' within, who converses with me the 'person'.

When you indiscriminately absorb all colours of life, then what is created is only blackness. Was I cleansing my insides by allowing life's sorrows and pains to come out?

The sorrows had been absorbed along with some colours, my metaphor for happiness.

In these verses, these thoughts get amalgamated with real life situations and experiences.

Words cannot lie, not such as those that fall right down from the sky.

Words that come rolling like thunder awoke me from slumber.

You may wish to share my light or you may wish for your own words.

All is not said till you light the midnight lamp at your own bedside.

Dear Kochi, many of these words and thoughts therein are for you.

1. Messenger

Whose call comes through strong winds?
The white messengers no longer sing
I struggle for want of my own wings.
The currents come on with sudden force
The shallow path lacks resource
Where depth and beauty exist there is no course.
The suddenness of revelation
The newness and rejuvenation
I jumped and swam to find simplification.
It was not wrathful, but forceful
It was beauty tangible
None stops if you are sufficiently wilful.

2. Birth

When you follow the sign
It takes you to where the stars shine
It is higher than all height
You are determined to show your might.
The crumbling sand hides a pristine lake
Or meadows that lovers take
All beings roam in this pasture
As there is sustenance from one to the other.
Illusions of one kind or another,
Searching for infinity caused your departure
Coming to this place of consciousness
You are a child of the child of sacrifices.
Glorious energy birthed a great teacher.

3. Sai

He exists only when you see
From the eyes of your mind
Or from the eyes on your skin
From the sight that comes from within.
He is gone the moment you speak
For you hear yourself not him,
He goes down spiralling into the schism
While your eyes look up to the form that was him.
His confusion a temporary dwelling
Your confusion is never-ending;
You seek to see but not hear his wailing
Whether here or there your liberation he is trying.

4. He...M

He said all religions are one.
We are flowers from the same garden
Why this little girl chose lavender?
When sunflowers abound and dahlias
All over majestic tree-dropped cotton.
Orange of the forest flaming
Everywhere her feet hopping
Cut not the trees which are our temples
Pray rather for their bloom and ageing.
Almond blossoms pure white in making
Translucent on autumn trees of fruiting
Her young heart on rough earth pounding
Is there more to find simply by wanting?
Left naked without leaf or bloom
Colours more, yellow and brown
Leaving an impression of doom
Hidden harshness huge looms.
Wheels turned once in demarcation
In this garden of flowers and religion
Nurture here, music, mystic and meditation.

5. Arrival

Children are borne
Each, parents given
Some with one and some none.
I found a child with all
Yet it went to another's house
They loved this odd soul.
It left another's house to yet anew
Its laughter and joy understood by few
What crooked painful bones the child grew.
Parent and child are one.
The song of this child fine
Echoes and rings with deep rhyme,
SAYS ALL ARE MINE.

6. Know my Tears

Where do I take my tears?
At whose feet will they fall?
Whose feet will receive
The sacred waters of my heart's call?
Know not these tears as sorrow
Know not them as pain
Know not as a beggars taunt
Only as love unfathomable.
For these waters are the melting snow
The growing warmth I am beginning to know
For you too, when you receive them seeing
The glow in the flow.
If in ignorance you let it pass
Lost it will be in waters vast
Muddied by banks, bodies, million feet and faces lost.
My tears clear and pure
With love will they touch feet, face, body, all.

7. Sense of Pleasure

When pleasures drenched the body
Every touch evoked more feeling
There was no foreboding
Unceasing the senses left you giddy.
Inner storms of such might
Some or all in part hurt
What gets lost is magic
Stripped thus yet not tragic.
Christ is now borne inside
You are wearing his crown
With thorns of stark reality
Bear it; this too shall pass shortly.

8. Question 2

How big is the ocean?
How deep its depth?
Is there a bottomless bottom?
Like the sky limitless?
Who lives in the sky?
Who lives on air?
Who can walk on water?
What can grow without soil?
HIMSELF he gives a reply,
I am not the last to question
I am the first to ask with my own intuition
Mine will not be the only revelation
For mystery and history are just timely illusions.

9. Vermillion

A few specks of the red vermillion
Decorates the small frame of her face
She was a virgin before she found her life-mate.
Man or woman how to differentiate?
Tied in a bond not to separate
Grow into each other or imitate.
Bonds of life cannot be forged
Time and space are larger than community's hold
Even burning coal in hours left cold.
Larger and stronger frames
Created in new designs and shapes
For a while to hold and integrate.
Hide and seek they alternate
Like dissolves like
Water alone will wash the stain.
HOLD and LOVE, as if nothing's at stake.

10. Buddha Purnima

Child devoted to many lives
Family, servants, siblings alike
Given to wild dreams and walks at night.
To him came the touch of light
The tender years of inner fight
Left when appeared his white knight.
Knight left behind a prince of might
Powers of unbound love now in him
One heart filled to the brim.
Love exploded the walls of prince's house
Relations, humanity filled, still there was more
Hunger and thirst altered not his heart's will.
He took a new walk to the hills.

11. Fake Yogi

I saw her sitting on the rock of salvation
Her alter-ego chasing her all the time
Ahead of her was standing he who was freedom
Though not free from shadows hers or his own.
She shied away from meeting him
She merged his shadow to her own
To union this she gave her voice and sight
Luminous energy too, leaving her with just a note.
Her music, her joy was her spirituality
She was no fake yogi.
Renouncing to her shadowy glitterati
She walked off the rocky top to obscurity.
Hidden from both twilight and sunny blaze
With steady steps and bright gaze
She sparkled against all illumination
It is an easy work of God to assail.

12. Love

Max was the one who found her
Maybe he was seeking to further his yoga
Though time for her was past such quests.
His hand reached out to her nape
Her baldness covered by no cape
Around her neck were small figures in a string of memory.
These were her people, morphed figures
Indistinguishable on her frame
Each like her own shrivelled fingers.
As he touched her they spread
Naked, dancing, embracing, joyously freed,
He unravelled them to gently shred.
She was his before this time came
Thus was he here now to hold her dying
To clear the past and present ties of her name.

13. Bees

I caught a honey bee before it stung
Searching for the queen I found her slave
His honey sweet and bite brave.
Many-a-days in their conclave
I brooded for when it will be the day
Soon buzz will be out in their grave.
Why this noiseless smoke in the orchard?
Is it for sensual fruit that they tortured?
Silent bystander to fate of those the trees nurtured.
When it was over it was
Burnt stumps and black dust,
Earth turned black, return must.
Who will bear the cost
Of rain gods and winds of gust?
I for one turned away eyes shut.
There was a gentle touch
Had I not known trust?
Earth with its own might will reconstruct.

14. Bloom 2

Long chain of stones or beads or pearls
Preciousness value in mind twirls
Outside a busy life unfurls.
Naked branches full of bunched pearls
Ready to burst any day into blooms
Squirrels running along natural tombs.
Life will come forth to change
Then shall I pick my chain to celebrate
Which decoration suits this priceless state?
Bird song and squirrel whispers is all it takes.

15. Unstill

At the cliff's edge started the nightly walk
The moon shone on the moss-covered rocks
At times she slept till the sun rose to shock.
Can thoughts be made to nought?
Why ask the question that is a mighty burden?
Listen rather to sounds that abound, to mind lighten.
The black tower of misplaced solace
Unformed knowledge trapped in its hollowness
Only the unstill voice of uncalmness.
Ocean roars must and do satisfy
Passionate thrust on walls to cries nullify
Forever truth that is, these cliff rocks testify.

16. A Hut

Unsown seed gave forth this tree
Like all others in this grove of trees
It loomed and spread above and below
To hide the haven of my abode.
My hut is a union of mud, water and grass
Leaves fall from the trees above
Showering as if with endless love
Unknowing, unfeeling, unliving at last.
A place that holds my attention
To live, move and obtain sustenance
I do have to abide by new rules
And persist in a life of unending blues.
What befalls or befell I endure
In this place, present habitat
I know not what will prevail and persist
So too thoughts in my heart fill.
Do I let in this quicksand, a ghostly blithe!

17. Clouds

Red blue clouds in the breeze
Silver lined against the light
Where in the mist secrets you freeze?
Sudden thunders energise and stir a tease.
Stealthy moves you well know
You change colour in one go
Orange, pink, white and yellow
So give to me my dear lover.
Dotted are planets next to you
Freely you float to unknown realms
But why cloud my vision of solar experience?
Or where from, this sudden élan in my existence?
Beauty is found anew mine
Breeze flows through senses nine
Thoughts and prayers soar high
Are you the lost lover divine?

18. Birds 1

Three little birdies snuggled
Sitting on a branch of thick wood
In musical chirpings and joyful sounds the air was filled.
Young chicks with tender feet
Grew strength with each feed,
Till stand they could to see the woods.
The sky was nothing beyond the trees
They pecked at each other for it was so peculiar
Nature had they knew not secured their nurture.
Their dismay gave way to wings
They learnt: with each flutter movement begins
To fly, fly back and to new nestlings.

19. Two Birds in Air

Together in flight
Every particle in step and sink
How did they learn to do this?
In a place where nothing is such as this.
Wings outstretched so too their necks
In search yet knowing what's next
Be it two or many, in silence or speech
Their journey puts others in context.
Timeless space without ruffles they define
Birds in a narrow confine,
Without any disturbing sign.
Restraining turbulence till the finish line.

20. Mirror

The air, the roadways, the streams and waterways
You walk on every way
The rituals and its healing
You use every day.
Do not question their worth
Of what you hold to debate
Those that very thoughts create
Only the gifted wear a pigtail.
The destitute is you if you do not share
If in poverty some lay bare
Money is only the fruit of mind's conception
Everyone a mirror for your reflection.

21. Roses

I bought myself some roses
And other flowers of lesser charm
Together they are worthy of a poet
I indulged in my personal vices.
Hymns to the gods or is it to my roses?
That hold every virtue you adore
You worship to the heavens eyes closed
But your senses receive their fading odour.
I behold the dying beauty in my hands
Tomorrow its essence will be in me.
I am neither strong nor rich
Yet in their softness I am embraced.
This is not an act of frivolity
Bear with my reverence
With its look of wanton triviality.

22. Ominous Sign

I find no reason for the ominous sign
For the rains have gone further ashore
To new realms or nowhere at all.
The muddy paths of my village
Dry and clear are, of snakes
In accordance with laws nature dictates.
Sun lurks behind gone is the heat
Its radiance now diffuse
Leaves on trees hang as if bruised.
The clouds remain still
Laden dark without frills
Waiting to be gone before the chill.
In the very middle of a dark night
They will pass over this hill.

23. The Veil

She was in pain and her little one crying
Thus they came to engage in the world
Looking for intimacy in the growing space
All too soon lost was the liquid warmth.
In the best of giving spirit and care
Together rejoice they did
Neglect, abandonment, not to fear
Even when the darkness enveloped to scare.
The first words called for 'mother'
Broke the link in between further
There are stories, lullabies and promises
But a better world will never be hither.
The womb is an oppressive place not
What of its nurture one cannot picture
But the smile was there before exposure
This and serenity a veil of secretive pleasure.

24. My Love

Emerging into unavoidable disclosure
I had in me the secret world
I inherited it unknown even to her
Whose womb for nine months me bore.
I carried a bag full of secrets
It could not be understood by slang or argots
Was it civilised by care?
They repeatedly asked her with each passing year.
I saw her hands were always engaged
It was for bed and bread she kneaded
With heart heavy of desires not revealed
My eyes to her pleaded.
Where was I conceived and for where?
I recognise no place belong nowhere
No need for this shelter
I just want to birth in you over and over.

25. Umbilical Cord

In this cord of unison is my music
Cut not that which is my essence
For I can survive not even a while
Remove if you will through which I nourish.
Like all cords with two ends
Mine too found double favour
I am there exactly where you left
My hand holding yours in continuous endeavour.
I hear much chatter but nothing to endear
Or tear me asunder in laughter
Or delight and pleasure in worldly wonder
When you left, you made a blunder.
I am old now and the cord still there
It is morphed, mushy and filth-ridden
What changed it is not for me to explain
What you left come back to reclaim.
Tomorrow's the dawn of my reincarnation
Be it not in pain.

26. Ma

Her name was goddess
And I, her only one
Born to her who was perfection.
She held my fascination
I knew she was no incarnation
Flowers at her feet while I at bosom.
Hearing that her real power was in leaving me
She replied her power was rather in giving
Hugging me while these thoughts kept unfolding.
Come caretaker, father and all
Connections to material and immaterial
Her power of giving immeasurable.

27. Defense

Round and round the football field
Many times he stopped to ponder
Looking for a way while about to wander
Sighting the goal post he took to shield.
He was strong and got the ball overrun
Pushed around I often came undone
He defended his team in the humdrum
All day all night the game was on.
Laughing in the field adds a new dimension
Arguments, altercations part of the preparation
I kicked too but only his feet curved the ball in motion
His header focussed my head disjointed by action ~
The years didn't pass in gloom
A faint-hearted I didn't groom
A goal, a swinger, all in the same pitch
In our warm hearts the only referee to hitch.

28. A New Her

What comes after birth?
After it is all over?
When the cord is cut and thrown?
Her fluids all washed off your bone?
The tenderness inside of her
Is beyond all measure
Did you say blood brother?
A blind truth which lies dear.
There has to be only one
Love and sustenance through whom sown.
She who needs to be known
Who waded through life's myriad tones.
As she waits for her turn
Unaware the music changes to a monotone
Leaving guests left her a fading hue
Singing in the nest the only symphony she knew.

29. A Story

Here is a story to tell like any other
Set in mountainous valleys
Such beauty words describe tirelessly.
If pictures can tell all why describe
Memory is a film negative of your sight
In perfectionist beauty appears a blight.
Always under darkness of clouds
Or wrapped in transparent mist
I asked my flighty friends for a gist.
Replied, it is black/green and thick with forest
Softest rain fills leaving nothing untouched
The valley soaks in delight when you rest.
Varied stories intertwine many truths
I create a picture by transference
And curl-up in the dream-works of my companions.

30. Soft Cotton

Gentle breeze of mid-day summer
In it the pure whiteness of feather
Come down from the skies as shower
Wandering clouds freed from owner.
So soft and tender cotton
Held on to the atmosphere
Challenging in ways rare
For air is weightless do compare.
You fruit from trees common
Your heart in centre so open
In bewitching manner you call attention
Temporary carpet on road of impressions!
Love and presence so ephemeral oh fugitive father...

31. Tigress

She was a tigress but not cruel
Her long uniform stripes to some distasteful
She chose to display it grandly
For to such a life she was grateful.
She chased her prey in play
She also preyed to kill
Her stripes never changed colour
But some thought one day it will.
In her life there was good and evil.
Let me rewind to what had come to pass
Her cubs she fed to their fill
Each day a new flavour till one day
She left them at the dead elephant carcass.
Before the mid-morning heat she was gone
At water's edge they kept playing till dawn
Many players come here thirst drawn
Amongst them the cubs learnt to carry on.
For she was a tigress of wilderness not culture born.

32. Walk on Water

Holding his hands
Like walking on water!
For hardly anyone possible
But for one solitary it is a slider.
The whitely white clouds
Come towards where I stood
Making plausible my seaward journey
Ahead in stealth and changing tide the sea is dreary.
The pythoness of dark clouds
The ocean edge of deep forest
In between is my rocking boat of obstinacy
Holding oar, fish line and all life's prophecies.
It is on reaching the very edge and finality
Nature rejoices of a union not in pity
Coming off a rough ride through all life's hypocrisies.

33. Kali

Men and women climbed onto the feet
Crawled onto it to investigate
Whose feet were they?
Not given to fear they opened their mind's gate.
She did not come from their land
She came from the edge of the earth
The horizons that the living abandoned
Her heritage, the boundary of heaviness and mirth.
They washed, cleaned and painted her
Red colour made the feet more human
Formed an image on every doorstep
In each hut every night summoned.
She could not explain her presence
The reason for her shame and lost eminence
The Lord's word given to her she distributed
They had not lost whom they yesterday cremated.
Dancing her dance of love and destruction she departed.

34. Shivaratri

Aarti of flowers and fire
Milk and water of my desire
I give to you with bells ringing in rear.
Raw milk of pristine whiteness
With plunging force leaving a veil
Now surrounded by dry leaves of pureness.
I give to you my raw faith
I crawl, prowl and circulate
My feet washed in the milk you eliminate.
For I needed to shake off the sand
Purify the body that I damned
And which my soul abandoned.

35. Fable of the Tree-Man

It is beautiful, intricate, but just a fable
Told in strange ways of Man's annals.
Of journeys he remembered and also forgot
Of unexplored gardens of what more could be got.
It is too long a time to chronicle
For what he thought to you tell.
He may indeed have been a weeping willow
He at times felt like a plantain dear fellow.
Like whispers in the wind he speaks
And rustles too with the leaves.
Someone, whose evolution was from the trees!

36. Myth in Durga's Life

Fables from time immemorial
Tell me of no ancestors
No great and grand mothers and fathers
Rather they tell of timeless immortals.
Parables as these have only creation
Changeable without extinction
A story you may shout is only myth
I scream back in a still pool of objection.
I grew up in an epic way
No age can define my stay
Amongst such that is bountiful
Amongst nature that is plentiful.
Keep your mythical fable
For I too have reached that pedestal.

37. Ganga

You gave Bhishm away
You still glow
In the mid-noon sun and under the moon
The world comes to you yet you flow.
A long blue pool is left by the wayside
By your overpowering steely shimmer
Everything you touch turns golden
Even the mound of rocks strewn aside.
You are building a palace
For elaborate and intricate is the rocky mound
Coming up as walls I see around
You I think will shed your flimsy gown.
It is not the sea but earth you want
Not the sky but mountains you wish to haunt
When the curse of building and providing is over
You will ravage in a deep ravine much drier.
Some may yet see you in nether land
Who caught not your sight in mainlands?
You are a legend once in demand
But you claimed your life into your own hands.

38. Pleasure Pot

A pot full of delectable ingredients
So large that none could go beyond it
Other pots, smaller and in varied colours
Remained unopened like mute markers.
This largest was a pleasure pot
That filled each mouth to satiate
Some even fell into it in haste
Crawling in and out, each time for a fresh taste.
Eventually was found a way
Pleasure for all to partake
In portions and parts to allocate
For the goddess likes well-behaved play.
Her steady, slant, downward cast eyes saw
Hands still bereft of her bounty
Mouths that had not tasted her sweetness
Eyes tired of waiting and wanting to be happy.
There are many lacking in prosperity
Although with her comes plenty
Bless not only spiritual piety

We all are instruments of her gaiety.
She comes with her trident
Each year be of that confident
Let it remain in the heart of the demon
Loose not her bejewelled hands of entertainment.
Till the sun gives light and shade,
The pleasure pot will bestow and cede
For sharing is the highest of all creed
Slavery to want lets the devil breed.

39. Spider's Mark

She made me cry
Said serves you right
I had just hit my target
Felled stack of stones reflecting my plight.
If I can fly a kite
Keep it floating hours in delight
With a cheering squad by my side
Why does she still prayers recite?
Some things come without a warning sign
Her beauty was indeed pristine
As you could not see the spider mark behind
The spider's attack and bite happened when she was nine.
Temporary tattoos as anointment
Decorated hands and feet in sacrament
She left me to experience everything
Stopping me at the brink of fulfillment.
The spider has not just left his mark
Into his web he had her wedded
The disappearing tattoos

Left her with the scar further embedded.
If you think I am wrong
Can you at least tell me a happy story
Her story of places far flung
Her misguided rosary kept her in mute unsound.
She made me...cry
Had I the washcloth wrung?

40. Birthday Wish

Who is interested in this tale?
They know you eat fish
You on occasion laugh but seldom smile
You always make a birthday wish.
For wellness and fullness
Of people with want and need
Standing at the temple gates
Where gargoyles stare down in seeming greed.
The best and biggest smiles are under these gates
In faces which are varied caricatures of fate
This is the most famous of all gates
Ambaal fed me here just enough.
Then she read my writings on the slate.
It is a temple and a state
Where mind matters and the inner-self dominates,
Citizens speak of the ruling laws
Allowing barriers of expression to break.
Here you will not see lazy loiter
Freedom of spirit here is graded backwards

Making children an illusory clutter
Exchange of energies between child and aged occur.
This temple tale of my existential flavour
Is a mix of right and wrong ingredients
Made of coveted thoughts and odd behaviour
In the long run functional all together.

41. Great Fools

I tried to use Fevicol
To hold the string into the wedge
Even though cut strings can only be knotted.
In this venture to rejoin
There is freshness of new inquisitiveness
Some will mix, match and recombine
What others will think foolishness.
When fools come to live with commoners
They bring their own worldliness
Their jest used where there is need to apologise
Happiest of all live in fool's paradise.
Normalcy exists not without contraptions
Fevicol and other inventions are their dependence
Constructing anything needs pre-conception
Even the greatest fools make a contribution.

42. Invisible Cloak

I recall the day
On which the metro came, was opened
Noiselessly shedding its various covers
The same day my father got a black coat.
This invisibility coat was a gift
He wore it saying it had been a long wait
Of course I never saw him again
From my window I at least saw the metro train.
Of the many ice-creams from ice-wallahs
And rickshaw rides from the station
Thoughts amaze when they come as memories
This metro is better than my first toy train.
The invisibility cloak of patriarchy from birth
Ensured I never needed to prove my worth
The father's poor invisibility coat passed down generations
Without ever finding parent, father or even simply a shirt!

43. Mad Fool

Madness is not foolishness
Foolishness may or may not be madness
Into my mind's eye I look in earnest
Removing each stitch, one by one.
Answers may lie in soul's nakedness
I remember the pregnant rat in my dissection
Mice would have been better for these experiments
Foolishness of choice making it amiss.
Madness often gets asylum
Fools only dismissed
Practising foolishness can be dumb
Given a choice which would I become?
This quest is quite abstract
Foolishness does not attract
If you can add, multiply and subtract
Even with such gifts I may be mad.
Absurd comparisons are not incorrect
Part can be larger than the whole
The mind is greater than my body
Mind is even greater than the SOUL.